Get Familiar With Pakistani Cooking

The Complete Guide to Pakistani Dishes for Beginners

BY: Valeria Ray

License Notes

Copyright © 2019 Valeria Ray All Rights Reserved

All rights to the content of this book are reserved by the Author without exception unless permission is given stating otherwise.

The Author have no claims as to the authenticity of the content and the Reader bears all responsibility and risk when following the content. The Author is not liable for any reparations, damages, accidents, injuries or other incidents occurring from the Reader following all or part of this publication.

A Special Reward for Purchasing My Book!

Thank you, cherished reader, for purchasing my book and taking the time to read it. As a special reward for your decision, I would like to offer a gift of free and discounted books directly to your inbox. All you need to do is fill in the box below with your email address and name to start getting amazing offers in the comfort of your own home. You will never miss an offer because a reminder will be sent to you. Never miss a deal and get great deals without having to leave the house! Subscribe now and start saving!

https://valeria-ray.gr8.com

Contents

Delicious Pakistani Food Recipes 6

(1) Dahi Puri 7

(2) Pakistani Seekh Kebabs 10

(3) Authentic Moong Dal 13

(4) Pakistani Chicken Biryani 17

(5) Curried Pasta 22

(6) Pakistani Tomato Salad 26

(7) Pakistani Dynamite Chicken 28

(8) Chicken Karahi Qeema 32

(9) Matar Keema 35

(10) Traditional Chicken Tikka 38

(11) Pakistani Methi Chicken 41

(12) Almond Meatballs 45

(13) Haleem 49

(14) Pakistani Sweet Gulab Jamun 53

(15) Pakistani Beef and Potato Curry 56

(16) Rice and Goat Curry 59

(17) Traditional Besan Ladoo 63

(18) Pakistani Lamb Koftas 65

(19) Aloo Gohst 68

(20) Pakistani Batter Potatoes 71

(21) Pakistani Potato Cakes 74

(22) Mint Chutney 77

(23) Classic Buttered Chicken 79

(24) Chicken Karahi 82

(25) Pakistani Samosas 85

About the Author 88

Author's Afterthoughts 90

Delicious Pakistani Food Recipes

MMMMMMMMMMMMMMMMMMMMMMMMMMMMM

(1) Dahi Puri

This is another traditional Pakistani dish that is nearly impossible to resist. Make this whenever you need to serve something classy to your significant other.

Yield: 2 servings

Cooking Time: 10 minutes

List of Ingredients:

- 14 homemade puffed puris
- 1/3 cup of Moong sprouts, stems removed
- 2 potatoes, boiled, peeled and chopped into small pieces
- 1 onion, chopped
- ¼ cup of coriander, chopped
- 1/3 cup of sev, fine
- 1 ½ cups of curd, thick
- 2 to 3 Tablespoons of white sugar
- ¼ cup of Kharjur chutney
- ¼ cup of green chutney
- 1 tablespoon of powdered cumin
- 1 teaspoon of powdered red chili
- 1 teaspoon of chaat masala
- Dash of salt

MMMMMMMMMMMMMMMMMMMMMMMMMMMM

Methods:

1. Steam the Moong sprouts with a dash of salt for 5 minutes or until soft.

2. In a bowl, add in the white sugar, thick curds, dash of salt and 1 teaspoon of the powdered cumin. Beat on the highest setting until smooth in consistency.

3. Poke small holes in the puris and place onto 2 plates.

4. Fill the puris with ½ teaspoon of the moong sprouts. Fill also with 1 teaspoon of the potatoes pieces and chopped onion. Add in a dash of the Kharjur chutney and green chutney. Add 3 to 4 tablespoons of the beaten curd mix.

5. Pour the remaining curd mix over the puris.

6. Serve with a garnish of powdered cumin, powdered red chili, chaat masala and dash of salt.

(2) Pakistani Seekh Kebabs

This is another snack dish I know you will want to make as often as possible. Serve this dish with a fresh salad or rice for the best results.

Yield: 4 servings

Cooking Time: 15 minutes

List of Ingredients:

- ½ pound of lamb, minced
- 1 ½ teaspoons of salt
- 1 teaspoon of powdered red chili
- 4 green chilies, chopped
- 1 handful of coriander, chopped
- 2 onions, peeled and thinly sliced
- 1, 2-inch piece of ginger, peeled
- 1 tablespoon of coriander seeds
- 1 tablespoon of cumin seeds
- Vegetable oil, for frying

MMMMMMMMMMMMMMMMMMMMMMMMMMMMMMM

Methods:

1. In a frying pan, add in the coriander and cumin seeds. Cook for 1 to 2 minutes or until toasted. Transfer into a mortar and pestle and crush until finely ground.

2. In a food processor, add in the onions, peeled ginger, chopped green chilies and coriander. Pulse on the highest setting until thoroughly chopped.

3. Add in the crushed seeds, minced lamb, dash of salt and powdered chili to the food processor. Pulse again until fine in consistency. Transfer into a bowl.

4. Knead the mix with your hands. Shape into thin kebabs.

5. In a frying pan set over medium to high heat, add in the vegetable oil. Add in the kebabs. Fry for 5 minutes or until gold.

6. Remove and drain. Serve immediately.

(3) Authentic Moong Dal

This is a common and authentic Pakistani dish that is typically served on an everyday basis in Pakistan. Typically served with hot rice, this is a filling and delicious dish I know you will love.

Yield: 4 servings

Cooking Time: 1 hour

List of Ingredients:

- 2 cups of dried yellow split peas
- 1 cup of tomatoes, chopped
- 1 onion, thinly sliced
- 1 teaspoon of powdered red chili
- ½ teaspoons of powdered coriander
- ½ teaspoons of powdered turmeric
- Dash of black pepper
- 3 cloves, whole
- 2 pods of cardamom
- 1 bay leaf
- 4 leaves of curry
- 1 teaspoon of powdered garam masala
- 2 Tablespoons of lemon juice
- 2 cloves of garlic, thinly sliced
- ½ teaspoons of garlic paste
- ½ teaspoons of ground cumin
- 2 dried red chili peppers
- 2 Tablespoons of coriander leaves, chopped
- 2 green chilies, chopped
- Dash of salt
- 3 Tablespoons of ghee
- 1 tablespoon of vegetable oil

Methods:

1. Wash the dried split peas under running water. Transfer into a bowl and cover with water. Allow to soak for 30 to 35 minutes.

2. In a saucepan set over medium to high heat, add in the drained split peas, powdered red chili, powdered coriander, powdered turmeric and garlic paste. Stir well to mix and allow to come to a boil. Cook for 10 to 12 minutes.

3. Add in the chopped tomatoes and chopped green chilies. Cook for 10 minutes or until soft.

4. Add in the bay leaves, fresh lemon juice, dash of salt and powdered garam masala. Stir well to mix.

5. In a saucepan set over medium to high heat, add in the vegetable oil, add in the sliced onion. Cook for 5 minutes or until gold.

6. In a separate skillet, add in the ghee. Add in the cumin seeds, whole cloves, dash of black pepper, pods of cardamom, chopped curry leaves, red chilies and garlic. Stir well to mix. Cook for 5 minutes.

7. Remove from heat and serve with a garnish of chopped coriander.

(4) Pakistani Chicken Biryani

If you are looking for a delicious dish that will explode in your mouth with a variety of different flavors, then this is the perfect dish for you to prepare.

Yield: 6 servings

Cooking Time: 2 hours

Ingredients for the onions:

- 5 onions, peeled and thinly sliced
- ¼ cup of vegetable oil, for frying

Ingredients for the chicken:

- 2.2 pounds of chicken, cut into small pieces
- 1, 2-inch piece of papaya
- ½ cup of beaten yogurt
- ½ inch piece of ginger, minced
- 3 cloves of garlic, minced
- 1 ½ Tablespoons of powdered red chili
- 1 teaspoon of powdered turmeric
- 1 teaspoon of garam masala

Ingredients for the masala:

- 5 Tablespoons of butter
- 1 teaspoon of crushed red pepper flakes
- 2 teaspoons of powdered garam masala
- 3 cloves of garlic, whole
- 1, 1-inch piece of ginger
- 4 green chilies, chopped
- 1 teaspoon of powdered turmeric
- ¼ teaspoons of black peppercorns, whole
- 2 Tablespoons of whole garam masala
- 4 tomatoes, chopped
- ¼ cup of beaten yogurt
- ½ of a lemon, juice only
- ½ cup + ¼ cup of mint leaves, chopped and for garnish
- Dash of salt

Ingredients for the rice:

- 2 ½ cups of basmati rice, soaked for 30 minutes and drained
- ½ teaspoons of cumin seeds
- 4 bay leaves
- 2 black peppercorns, whole
- 10 pods of green cardamom
- Whole cloves
- 1 stick of cinnamon
- 3 pods of black cardamom
- ½ teaspoons of saffron threads
- ¼ teaspoons of rose essence
- Dash of salt

MMMMMMMMMMMMMMMMMMMMMMMMMMMMMM

Methods:

1. Prepare the onions. In a skillet set over high heat, add in the oil. Add in the sliced onions and cook for 20 to 25 minutes or until caramelized. Remove and transfer onto a plate lined with paper towels to drain.

2. Prepare the chicken. In a bowl, add in all of the ingredients for the chicken. Stir well to mix. Cover and set aside to marinate for 30 minutes to 1 hour.

3. Prepare the masala. In a food processor, add in the ginger, garlic cloves and green chilies. Pulse on the highest setting until a coarse paste begins to form. Remove and set aside.

4. In a skillet set over high heat, add in the butter. Add in the powdered masala, crushed red pepper flakes, powdered turmeric, black peppercorns, and whole garam masala. Stir well to mix. Add in the garlic and ginger paste and chopped tomatoes. Stir well to mix. Cook for 5 minutes or until aromatic.

5. Add in the chicken and season with a dash of salt. Cook for 5 minutes. Lower the heat to medium and continue to cook for 15 minutes or until the chicken is soft.

6. Prepare the rice. Drain the rice and place into a saucepan with 4 cups of water. Add in the cumin seeds and remaining ingredients. Stir well to mix. Set over medium to high heat and allow to come to a boil. Lower the heat to low and cook for 20 minutes or until all of the water has been absorbed.

7. Transfer the cooked chicken to the saucepan with the rice. Top off with the masala.

8. Cover and allow to steam over low heat for 8 minutes.

9. Remove from heat and serve immediately with a garnish of chopped mint and chopped cilantro.

(5) Curried Pasta

This is a deliciously spicy dish you can make whenever you are craving something spicy or whenever you are craving some Italian cuisine.

Yield: 4 servings

Cooking Time: 50 minutes

List of Ingredients:

- ¼ cup of chickpea flour
- 4 red bell peppers, seeds removed and chopped
- 3 curry leaves
- 1 pound of chicken, boneless, skinless and cut into small cubes
- 1 tablespoon of ginger and garlic paste
- 1 teaspoon of powdered turmeric
- 2 teaspoons of hot paprika
- ¼ cup of warm water
- 1, 2-ounce pack of powdered coconut milk
- 1 cup of water
- 1, 16-ounce box of spaghetti
- 3 green chile peppers, sliced thinly
- ½ cup of cilantro, chopped
- 1 lemon, sliced into thin slices

MMMMMMMMMMMMMMMMMMMMMMMMMMMMMMMM

Methods:

1. In a skillet set over medium to high heat, add in the chickpea flour. Cook for 5 minutes or until the flour is dark. Remove from heat and transfer into a bowl. Set aside to cool completely.

2. In a separate skillet set over medium to high heat, add in the chopped red bell peppers and curry leaves.

3. Add in the chicken cubes. Continue to cook for 5 minutes or until cooked.

4. Add in the garlic and ginger paste. Cook for another 30 seconds.

5. In the bowl with the chickpea flour, add in the powdered turmeric and cayenne pepper. Stir well to mix. Sprinkle into the skillet with the chicken. Stir well to coat and cook for 2 minutes.

6. Add in ¼ cup of the water into the skillet and deglaze the bottom of the skillet. Add in the powdered coconut milk and 1 cup of water. Stir well until the milk dissolves.

7. Lower the heat to low.

8. Prepare the spaghetti according to the directions on the package. Once cooked, drain the pasta and divide into serving bowls.

9. Pour the chicken mix over the top.

10. Serve immediately with a garnish of green chile pepper rings, chopped cilantro and thin lemon sliced.

(6) Pakistani Tomato Salad

Make this delicious salad dish whenever you need something on the fresh side. Best of all, you don't need to feel guilty about enjoying this salad.

Yield: 4 servings

Cooking Time: 10 minutes

List of Ingredients:

- 1 tablespoon of lemon juice
- 2 Tablespoons of vegetable oil
- ½ teaspoons of powdered cumin
- 4 tomatoes, chopped
- 1 cucumber, chopped
- ½ of a red onion, thinly sliced
- 1 red chili, thinly sliced

Methods:

1. In a bowl, add in the lemon juice, vegetable oil and powdered cumin. Whisk until mixed.

2. Season with a dash of salt and black pepper.

3. In a separate bowl, add in the chopped tomatoes, chopped cucumber, red onion and red chili. Toss well to mix.

4. Pour the dressing over the top and toss well until coated.

5. Serve immediately.

(7) Pakistani Dynamite Chicken

This is another savory Pakistani chicken dish that you will love especially if you love the taste of all things spicy.

Yield: 4 servings

Cooking Time: 20 minutes

Ingredients for the chicken:

- 2 Tablespoons of all-purpose flour
- 1 tablespoon of cornstarch
- 1 tablespoon of powdered red chili
- 1 tablespoon of ginger and garlic paste
- 1 egg, beaten
- ½ teaspoons of powdered cumin
- ½ teaspoons of garam masala
- ½ teaspoons of powdered coriander
- 1 teaspoon of soya sauce
- 1 tablespoon of lemon juice
- 2 to 3 drops of red food coloring, optional
- Dash of salt
- 3 pounds of chicken, boneless and cut into small cubes
- 1 teaspoon of rice flour
- Vegetable oil, for frying

Ingredients for tempering:

- 1 tablespoon of vegetable oil
- 1 teaspoon of mustard seeds
- Sprig of curry leaves
- ½ teaspoons of crushed red chili flakes

Ingredients for the sauce:

- ¼ cup of mayonnaise
- ½ teaspoons of powdered red chili
- 1 tablespoon of honey
- ½ teaspoons of mustard sauce
- 1 clove of garlic, grated
- 1 tablespoon of sweet sriracha
- 1 teaspoon of coriander leaves, chopped
- Dash of salt

MMMMMMMMMMMMMMMMMMMMMMMMMMMMMMM

Methods:

1. Prepare the chicken. In a bowl, add in all of the ingredients for the chicken, including the chicken. Do not add the vegetable oil and rice flour. Stir well to mix. Cover and set this mix into the fridge to chill for 3 to 4 hours.

2. Add in the rice flour and stir well until evenly incorporate.

3. In a pot, add in 2 to 3 inches of vegetable oil. Set over medium to high heat. Add in the chicken and fry for 8 to 10 minutes or until gold. Remove and drain on a plate lined with paper towels.

4. In a saucepan set over low to medium heat, add in the mustard seeds and 1 tablespoon of vegetable oil. Cook for 30 seconds before adding in the sprig of curry leaves and crushed red chili flakes. Stir well to mix and continue to cook for an additional 30 seconds.

5. Add the fried chicken to the saucepan. Toss to coat.

6. In a bowl, add in all of the ingredients for the sauce. Stir well to mix.

7. Transfer the chicken into a separate bowl. Pour the sauce over the chicken and toss well to coat evenly.

8. Serve immediately.

(8) Chicken Karahi Qeema

This is a delicious stir-fried chicken recipe I know you will love. One bite and I guarantee you will become hooked.

Yield: 4 servings

Cooking Time: 20 minutes

List of Ingredients:

- 1 pound of ground chicken
- ½ teaspoons of nigella seeds
- 1 tablespoon of ground garlic
- 1 tablespoon of ginger, minced
- 4 to 5 tomatoes, chopped
- 1 teaspoon of salt
- 1 ½ teaspoons of powdered red chili
- 1 ½ teaspoons of powdered coriander
- 1 teaspoon of powdered garam masala
- 3 to 6 green chilies, thinly sliced
- 1 handful of cilantro, chopped
- Lemon juice, juiced, optional and for serving

MMMMMMMMMMMMMMMMMMMMMMMMMMMMMM

Methods:

1. In a wok set over medium to high heat, add in a tablespoon of vegetable oil. Add in the nigella seeds and cook for 30 seconds.

2. Add in the ground garlic and minced ginger. Stir well to mix. Cook for an additional minute.

3. Add in the ground chicken, powdered red chili, dash of salt, powdered coriander and powdered garam masala. Stir well to mix. Cook for 8 to 10 minutes or until the chicken is brown.

4. Add in the chopped tomatoes. Continue to cook for 5 minutes or until soft.

5. Increase the heat to high. Continue to cook for 1 to 2 minutes or until dried.

6. Remove from heat. Serve with a garnish of sliced green chilies and lemon juice over the top.

(9) Matar Keema

This is an authentic Pakistani dish you can make whenever you are craving Pakistani cuisine. Made with authentic Pakistani ingredients, this is a dish I know you will love to make.

Yield: 4 to 5 servings

Cooking Time: 20 minutes

List of Ingredients:

- 1 cup of matar
- pounds of beef, minced
- tomatoes, chopped
- 1 onion, thinly sliced
- 6 Tablespoons of vegetable oil
- Dash of black pepper
- 1 pod of black cardamom
- ¼ teaspoons of cumin seeds
- 1 teaspoon of powdered coriander
- 1 teaspoon of salt
- ¼ teaspoons of powdered turmeric
- ¾ teaspoons of powdered chili
- 1 teaspoon of ginger paste
- 1 teaspoon of garlic paste
- ½ teaspoons of powdered garam masala

MMMMMMMMMMMMMMMMMMMMMMMMMMMM

Methods:

1. In a skillet set over medium to high heat, add in a spoonful of vegetable oil. Add in the sliced onions. Cook for 5 minutes or until brown.

2. Add in the chopped tomatoes, dash of black pepper, pod of black cardamom, cumin seeds, powdered coriander, dash of salt, powdered turmeric, powdered chili, ginger paste, garlic paste and powdered garam masala. Stir well to mix. Cook for 5 minutes or until soft.

3. Add in 2 cups of water, minced beef and matar. Cover and continue to cook for 10 minutes or until the meat is soft.

4. Remove from heat. Serve immediately.

(10) Traditional Chicken Tikka

This is another delicious dinner dish you can make any night of the week. Serve with steamed basmati rice for the best results.

Yield: 2 to 3 servings

Cooking Time: 1 hour

List of Ingredients:

- 1 pound of chicken, cut into pieces
- 1 ½ teaspoons of ginger paste
- 1 ½ teaspoons of garlic paste
- 1 bunch of coriander leaves, chopped
- 3 to 4 green chiles
- 1 onion, chopped
- 1 teaspoon of garam masala
- 4 to 5 dried chilies
- ½ teaspoons of salt
- 6 Tablespoons of yogurt

MMMMMMMMMMMMMMMMMMMMMMMMMMMMMM

Methods:

1. In a bowl, add in the ginger paste, garlic paste, green chilies, chopped onion, garam masala, dried chilies, dash of salt yogurt and chopped coriander leaves. Transfer into a food processor. Pulse on the highest setting until paste like in consistency.

2. Make 3 to 4 slits on each piece of chicken. Place into a bowl and pour the paste over the top. Toss well until coated.

3. Preheat the oven to 375 degrees.

4. Place the chicken onto a baking sheet. Place into the oven to bake for 20 minutes while covered with a sheet of aluminum foil. Then remove the foil and continue to bake for 10 to 15 minutes or until cooked through.

5. Increase the temperature of the oven to 450 degrees. Continue to bake for 2 to 3 minutes or until dried.

6. Remove and rest for 10 minutes before serving.

(11) Pakistani Methi Chicken

This is a restaurant quality Pakistani dish that is not only incredibly easy to make, but with it being made with fresh herbs, it is one of the tastiest dishes you will have the opportunity to make.

Yield: 4 servings

Cooking Time: 20 minutes

List of Ingredients:

- 1 pound of chicken bones, cut into pieces
- 2 cups of fenugreek, chopped
- ¾ cup of yogurt, whisked until smooth
- 3 tomatoes, chopped
- 2 onions, chopped
- 10 cloves of garlic, chopped
- 1, 2 inch piece of ginger, grated
- 3 to 4 green chilies, chopped
- 1 ½ teaspoons of powdered red chili
- 1 ½ teaspoons of powdered coriander
- ½ teaspoons of powdered turmeric
- 1 teaspoon of powdered garam masala
- 1 teaspoon of cumin seed
- 2 teaspoons of lemon juice, 1 teaspoon of white sugar
- 5 Tablespoons of vegetable oil
- Dash of salt
- Warm water, as needed
- 4 pods of green cardamom
- 8 to 10 whole peppercorns
- ½ teaspoons of mace, crushed
- 4 cloves, whole

Methods:

1. In a saucepan set over medium to high heat, add in the vegetable oil. Add in the cumin seeds and cook for 30 seconds or until they begin to crackle.

2. Add in the onions. Increase the heat to high and cook for 1 minute.

3. Add in the pods of green cardamom, whole peppercorns, crushed mace and whole cloves. Stir well to mix. Cook for 5 minutes or until the onions are gold.

4. Add in the chicken bones, chopped tomatoes, chopped garlic and grated ginger. Stir well to mix. Cook for 2 minutes.

5. Lower the heat to low. Add in the whisked yogurt and stir well to incorporate.

6. Add in the powdered red chili, powdered turmeric, powdered coriander, powdered cumin and dash of salt. Add in the warm water. Stir well until evenly mixed. Cover and cook for 8 minutes or until the chicken is soft.

7. Add in the fenugreek, lemon juice, powdered garam masala and white sugar. Stir well to evenly incorporate. Cook for an additional 1 to 2 minutes.

8. Remove from heat and serve immediately.

(12) Almond Meatballs

If you love the taste of meatballs, then this is one Pakistani dish I know you won't be able to resist the moment you get a taste of it.

Yield: 6 servings

Cooking Time: 1 hour and 30 minutes

List of Ingredients:

- ½ teaspoons of saffron
- 1 pound of beef, minced
- 1 egg, beaten
- 1 onion, chopped
- ½ cup of coriander leaves, chopped
- 1, 3-inch piece of ginger, grated
- 1 ½ Tablespoons of garam masala
- ½ teaspoons of powdered chili
- 1 tablespoon of besan flour
- 30 almonds, blanched, soaked for 2 hours
- ¼ cup of vegetable oil, for frying
- Coriander leaves, for serving

Ingredients for the sauce:

- 3 Tablespoons of ghee
- 2 onions, thinly sliced
- 4 cloves of garlic, chopped
- 1 teaspoon of powdered turmeric
- 1 teaspoon of powdered cumin
- 5 tomatoes, chopped
- ½ cup of plain yogurt

Methods:

1. Prepare the meatballs. In a bowl, add in the saffron and 2 teaspoons of boiling water. Soak for 10 minutes or until soft.

2. In a separate bowl, add in the minced beef, beaten egg, chopped onion, coriander leaves, grated ginger, garam masala, powdered chili and dash of salt. Stir well until mixed. Add in the besan flour. Knead until smooth in consistency.

3. Divide the mix into 30 balls.

4. Make an indent in the balls and add an almond into each meatball. Place onto a baking sheet and cover. Place into the fridge to chill for 20 minutes.

5. In a frying pan set over medium to high heat, add in the vegetable oil. Add in the meatballs and cook for 5 minutes or until brown. Remove and drain on a plate lined with paper towels to drain.

6. Prepare the sauce. In a saucepan set over medium to high heat, add in the ghee. Add in the onion slices and garlic. Cook for 8 minutes or until gold.

7. Add in the powdered turmeric, powdered cumin, chopped tomatoes and plain yogurt. Stir well to mix and lower the heat to low. Cook for 10 minutes or until soft.

8. Add in the cooked meatballs. Add in a dash of salt and ½ cup of water. Stir gently to mix.

9. Allow to come to a boil. Lower the heat to low and cook for 10 minutes or until the meatballs are cooked.

10. Serve the meatballs with a garnish of coriander leaves and a drizzling of the curry sauce over the top.

(13) Haleem

This is the ultimate slow cooked meal that you can prepare whenever you are craving something exotic. Made with beef and lentils, this is a dish that will leave you feeling full for hours.

Yield: 8 servings

Cooking Time: 4 hours and 30 minutes

List of Ingredients:

- ½ cup of chana dal
- ½ cup of urid dal
- ½ cup of mung dal
- ½ cup of barley
- 1 pound of beef, cut into small pieces
- 2 Tablespoons of garlic, crushed
- ½ cup of wheat berries
- 2 Tablespoons of ginger, grated
- 10 ½ cups of water
- ¼ teaspoons of ground fenugreek
- 2 Tablespoons of ghee
- Dash of saffron, optional
- 1 tablespoon of powdered coriander
- 1 tablespoon of powdered cumin
- 1 tablespoon of powdered garam masala
- 1 teaspoon of powdered turmeric
- Dash of salt
- ½ cup of vegetable oil
- 2 onions, thinly sliced
- 1 tablespoon of garam masala

MMMMMMMMMMMMMMMMMMMMMMMMMMMMMM

Methods:

1. In a bowl, add in the chana dal, urid dal, mung dal and barley. Stir well to mix and cover with water. Set aside to soak overnight.

2. The next day, in a separate bowl add in the wheat berries and crush thoroughly. Cover with water and set aside to soak for 1 ½ hours.

3. In a saucepan set over medium to high heat, add in the grains, lentils, beef pieces, crushed garlic, grated ginger and water. Stir well to mix and allow to come to a boil. Lower the heat to low and cook for 2 hours.

4. Remove the bone from the meat and continue to cook for an additional hour.

5. Add in the ghee, saffron, ground fenugreek, powdered coriander, powdered cumin, powdered garam masala, powdered chili and powdered turmeric. Stir well to mix and season with a dash of salt. Cook for 1 hour or until thick in consistency.

6. In a frying pan set over medium to high heat, add in the oil. Add in the sliced onion. Cook for 10 to 15 minutes or until caramelized. Transfer into the stew and stir well to incorporate. Continue to cook for an additional 15 minutes.

7. Remove from heat and serve immediately with a garnish of the fried onions.

(14) Pakistani Sweet Gulab Jamun

This is a highly popular and traditional Pakistani dessert dish that you can make whenever you have a strong sweet tooth that needs to be satisfied.

Yield: 10 servings

Cooking Time: 20 minutes

Ingredients for the Gulab:

- 1 cup of powdered milk
- 2 Tablespoons of all-purpose flour
- 1 teaspoon of semolina
- 1 egg, beaten
- 1 teaspoon of baker's style baking powder

Ingredients for the sheera:

- 2 cups of water
- 2 cups of white sugar
- ¼ teaspoons of powdered green cardamom

MMMMMMMMMMMMMMMMMMMMMMMMMMMMMM

Methods:

1. Prepare the gulab. In a bowl, add in all of the ingredients for the gulab. Stir well until smooth in consistency.

2. Shape the mix into 15 to 20 balls. Set onto a plate.

3. In a frying pan, add 2 to 3 tablespoons of vegetable oil. Add in the balls. Fry for 5 minutes or until gold.

4. Prepare the sheera. In a separate saucepan, add in the water and white sugar. Whisk until mixed. Allow to come to a boil. Cook for 5 to 8 minutes or until syrupy in consistency. Add in the powdered green cardamom. Remove and set aside to cool.

5. Pour the sheera over the fried gulab. Toss until coated thoroughly.

6. Set aside to rest for 35 to 40 minutes before serving.

(15) Pakistani Beef and Potato Curry

This is a deliciously quintessential Pakistani dish that is a must have in many Pakistani households. Feel free to use bone-in or boneless meat depending on your personal preferences.

Yield: 4 to 6 servings

Cooking Time: 1 hour and 35 minutes

List of Ingredients:

- 1 pound of beef chunks, boneless
- 2 onions, chopped
- 1 tablespoon of garlic, crushed
- 1 tablespoon of ginger, crushed
- 1 to 2 teaspoons of powdered red chili
- 1/3 teaspoons of powdered turmeric
- 1 ½ teaspoons of salt
- 2 tomatoes, chopped
- 2 potatoes, cut into wedges
- ½ teaspoons of powdered garam masala
- 1 handful of cilantro, chopped
- Green chilies, chopped and for serving
- Lemon juice, as needed and for serving

MMMMMMMMMMMMMMMMMMMMMMMMMMMMMM

Methods:

1. In a pot set over medium to high heat, add in the boneless beef pieces, powdered red chili, chopped onion, crushed garlic, crushed ginger and dash of salt. Stir well to mix.

2. Add in 2 cups of hot water. Cover and allow to come to a boil. Lower the heat to low and cook for 45 minutes to 1 hour or until the meat is soft.

3. In a separate skillet set over medium to high heat, add in another tablespoon of vegetable oil. Add in the garam masala. Transfer into the pot and cook for 1 minute.

4. Add in 1 cup of water and the potato wedges. Stir well to mix and allow to come to a boil. Lower the heat to low. Cook for 20 to 30 minutes or until the potatoes are soft.

5. Remove from heat. Add in the chopped cilantro, chopped green chilies and fresh lemon juice. Stir well to incorporate and serve immediately.

(16) Rice and Goat Curry

This is a marvelous dish to make whenever you are craving something even more on the exotic side. Layered with plenty of rice, chopped tomato, mint leaves and almonds, everyone who tries it will love it.

Yield: 8 servings

Cooking Time: 2 hours and 45 minutes

List of Ingredients:

- 2 Tablespoons of ghee
- 1 onion, sliced
- 4 cups of basmati rice
- 2 teaspoons of saffron
- 1 tomato, chopped
- ¼ cup of coriander leaves
- ¼ cup of mint leaves
- 1 green chili, sliced
- 2 Tablespoons of sultanas
- 2 Tablespoons of blanched almonds, lightly toasted

Ingredients for the curry:

- ¼ cup of vegetable oil
- 2 onions, sliced
- 1-pound goat leg, bone-in
- 6 cloves of garlic, crushed
- 1, 3-inch piece of grated ginger
- 10 cloves, whole
- 6 pods of green cardamom
- 1 tablespoon of powdered chili
- 6 bay leaves
- 1 tablespoon of powdered coriander
- 1 tablespoon of powdered cumin
- ½ cup of plain yogurt

MMMMMMMMMMMMMMMMMMMMMMMMMMMMMMMM

Methods:

1. In a saucepan set over medium to high heat, add in the vegetable oil. Add in the sliced onions. Cook for 8 minutes or until gold.

2. Add in the goat leg, crushed garlic and grated ginger. Stir well to mix and cook for 5 minutes or until the meat is seared.

3. Add in the plain yogurt and 2 ¼ cups of warm water. Add in the saffron threads, coriander leaves, mint leaves and sliced green chili. Stir well to mix. Lower the heat to low and cook for 2 hours or until the meat is soft.

4. Season with a dash of salt. Remove from heat and set aside.

5. In a skillet set over medium to high heat, add in the ghee. Add in the remaining onion and cook for 8 minutes or until gold. Remove and place onto a plate lined with paper towels to drain.

6. Cover the rice with water and allow to soak for 30 minutes. Drain and transfer into a pot. Cover with salted water and allow to boil for 8 to 10 minutes or until fluffy. Remove and serve the rice among serving bowls.

7. Top off with the goat curry.

8. Serve with a topping of the chopped tomato, coriander leaves, mint leaves, sultanas and blanched almonds.

(17) Traditional Besan Ladoo

This is a traditional Pakistani treat you can make whenever you have a strong sweet tooth that needs to be satisfied.

Yield: 10 servings

Cooking Time: 2 hours and 45 minutes

List of Ingredients:

- ¾ cup of ghee
- 2 cups of chickpea flour
- ½ cup of sweet coconut, shredded
- 3 Tablespoons of ground almonds
- ½ cup of castor sugar
- ½ teaspoons of powdered cardamom

MMMMMMMMMMMMMMMMMMMMMMMMMMMMMM

Methods:

1. In a wok set over low heat, add in the ghee. Add in the chickpea flour. Cook for 10 minutes or until toasted.

2. Remove and allow to cool for 5 minutes.

3. In a coffee grinder or food processor, add in the shredded coconut. Grind until fine in consistency.

4. Add in the ground almonds, castor sugar, ground coconuts and powdered cardamom into the wok. Stir well to mix.

5. Shape the mix into balls that are 1 inch in diameter. Place onto a baking sheet.

6. Set aside to rest for 2 to 3 hours before serving.

(18) Pakistani Lamb Koftas

If you need an appetizer dish to serve to your friends and family during your next dinner or lunch event, then this is the perfect dish for you to make.

Yield: 16 servings

Cooking Time: 50 minutes

List of Ingredients:

- 1 pound of lamb, minced
- 1 onion, chopped
- 1 handful of coriander leaves, chopped
- ½ teaspoons of powdered chili
- ½ teaspoons of salt
- 1 egg, beaten
- 4 eggs, hard boiled and cut into halves

Ingredients for the masala:

- 1 onion, thinly sliced
- 6 cloves of garlic, chopped
- ½ teaspoons of salt
- ½ teaspoons of powdered hot chili
- ½ teaspoons of ground coriander
- 1, 1-inch piece of ginger, grated

MMMMMMMMMMMMMMMMMMMMMMMMMMMMMM

Methods:

1. Prepare the meatballs. In a bowl, add in the minced lamb, chopped onion, dash of salt, chopped coriander leaves and the beaten egg. Stir well using your hands until evenly mixed.

2. Form the mix into balls the size of golf balls. Roll in your hands until smooth in consistency.

3. Transfer into the fridge to chill for 10 minutes.

4. In a saucepan set over medium to high heat, add in 3 to 4 tablespoons of the vegetable oil. Add in the chopped onion and cook for 5 minutes. Add in the garlic and stir well to mix. Cook for an additional 5 minutes.

5. Add in 1 cup of water, dash of salt, ground coriander, powdered hot chili and grated ginger. Stir well to mix. Cover and cook for 10 minutes or until reduced.

6. Add in the meatballs. Lower the heat to low and cook for 20 minutes or until cooked through.

7. Add in the hard-boiled eggs and spoon the sauce over the top.

8. Remove and serve with a garnish of chopped coriander.

(19) Aloo Gohst

This is a dish that literally translates to potato lamb. It is a simple curry that is packed full of meat and potatoes, making a filling dish you can enjoy any night of the week.

Yield: 6 to 8 servings

Cooking Time: 1 hour and 45 minutes

List of Ingredients:

- 1 pound of mutton
- ½ pound of potatoes, peeled and cut into 1 inch sized pieces
- ¼ teaspoons of powdered turmeric
- 1 teaspoon of powdered chili
- 3 Tablespoons of powdered coriander
- 3 to 4 cups of water
- 2 to 3 onions, thinly sliced
- ½ cup of vegetable oil
- 1 tablespoon of ginger paste
- 1 teaspoon of garlic paste
- 1 teaspoon of powdered garam masala
- 6 to 8 whole cloves
- Dash of black pepper
- 2 pods of black cardamom
- 1 ½ teaspoons of salt
- 1 cup of coriander leaves, chopped
- 2 to 3 green chilies, chopped
- 1 to 2 lemons, sliced into wedges and for serving

MMMMMMMMMMMMMMMMMMMMMMMMMMMMMMMM

Methods:

1. In a skillet set over medium to high heat, add in a spoonful of vegetable oil. Add in the sliced onion and cook for 5 minutes or until browned.

2. Add in the powdered turmeric, powdered chili, garlic paste, ginger paste and dash of salt. Stir well to mix.

3. Add in the mutton and 3 to 4 cups of water. Cover and cook for 1 hour or until the mutton is soft.

4. Add in the potato pieces, powdered garam masala, whole cloves, pods of black cardamom and green chilies. Stir well to mix. Cook for 20 to 30 minutes or until the potatoes are soft.

5. Remove from heat and serve immediately with a garnish of chopped coriander leaves and lemon wedges.

(20) Pakistani Batter Potatoes

This is a completely different way to eat your potatoes and once you try it, this is going to be the only dish that you make whenever you are craving potatoes.

Yield: 8 servings

Cooking Time: 25 minutes

List of Ingredients:

- 1 quart of vegetable oil, for frying
- 1 ½ cups of gram flour
- 1 teaspoon of salt
- 1 teaspoon of cayenne pepper
- 1 teaspoon of cumin seeds
- ¼ teaspoons of baker's style baking powdered
- ½ cup of warm water
- 4 potatoes, peeled and thinly sliced

MMMMMMMMMMMMMMMMMMMMMMMMMMMMMMM

Methods:

1. In a deep fryer, heat up the vegetable oil until it reaches 375 degrees.

2. In a bowl, add in the gram flour, dash of salt, cayenne pepper, cumin seeds and baking powder. Stir well to mix.

3. Add in the warm water and continue to stir until thick in consistency.

4. Dip the thin potato slices into the batter. Transfer immediately into the hot oil.

5. Cook for 4 minutes or until gold. Remove and transfer onto a plate lined with paper towels to drain.

6. Serve.

(21) Pakistani Potato Cakes

This is a delicious snack recipe that you can serve whenever you need something quick to make to hold you over until your next meal.

Yield: 6 to 8 servings

Cooking Time: 30 minutes

List of Ingredients:

- 1 pound of Yukon potatoes, peeled
- 1 teaspoon of cumin seeds
- 2 shallots, minced
- 1 bunch of cilantro, chopped
- ½ teaspoons of red chili flakes
- ½ teaspoons of black pepper
- Dash of salt
- 3 eggs, beaten
- Canola oil, for frying

MMMMMMMMMMMMMMMMMMMMMMMMMMMMMM

Methods:

1. In a pot set over medium to high heat, fill halfway with water. Add in the potatoes and boil for 20 to 25 minutes or until soft. Drain the potatoes completely and set aside.

2. In a skillet set over medium to a high medium heat, add in the cumin seeds. Cook for 1 minute or until fragrant.

3. In a bowl, add in the potatoes. Mash with a potato masher until smooth in consistency.

4. In the bowl, add in the toasted cumin seeds, minced shallots, chopped cilantro and red chili flakes. Season with a dash of salt and black pepper. Stir well to mix.

5. Shape the mix into patties that are 2 ½ inches in size.

6. In a skillet set over low to medium heat, add in the canola oil. Dip the potato cakes in the eggs and add into the skillet. Cook for 5 minutes or until gold on both sides.

7. Remove and serve immediately.

(22) Mint Chutney

This is a dish that you can make whenever you need to suddenly prepare an exotic appetizer to serve at your next family gathering.

Yield: 2 servings

Cooking Time: 5 minutes

List of Ingredients:

- 2 bunches of mint leaves
- 1 tablespoon of red chili flakes
- ½ cup of pureed tamarind
- 1 teaspoon of salt
- 1 cup of plain yogurt

MMMMMMMMMMMMMMMMMMMMMMMMMMMMMMM

Methods:

1. In a food processor, add in the mint leaves, red chili flakes, pureed tamarind and dash of salt.

2. Pulse on the highest setting until smooth in consistency.

3. Transfer into a bowl. Add in the plain yogurt and stir well until evenly incorporated.

4. Serve with a garnish of extra mint leaves.

(23) Classic Buttered Chicken

If you want to serve a traditional Pakistani dish to your friends and family, then this is one dish you can't go wrong with.

Yield: 4 servings

Cooking Time: 1 hour and 10 minutes

List of Ingredients:

- ¼ pint of yogurt
- 2 ounces of ground almonds
- 1 ½ teaspoons of powdered chili
- ¼ teaspoons of crushed bay leaves
- ¼ teaspoons of ground cloves
- ¼ teaspoons of ground cinnamon
- 1 teaspoon of garam masala
- 4 pods of green cardamom
- 1 teaspoon of ginger pulp
- 1 teaspoon of garlic pulp
- 1, 14 ounce can of tomatoes, chopped
- Dash of salt
- 2 pounds of chicken, skinless and cut into small cubes
- 3 ounces of butter
- 1 tablespoon of corn oil
- 2 onions, thinly sliced
- 2 Tablespoons of coriander, chopped
- 4 Tablespoons of heavy whipping cream

MMMMMMMMMMMMMMMMMMMMMMMMMMMMMM

Methods:

1. In a bowl, add in the yogurt, ground almonds, crushed bay leaves, powdered chili, ground cloves, powdered cinnamon, garam masala, pods of green cardamom, ginger pulp, and garlic pulp. Stir well until evenly mixed.

2. Add in the chicken and toss well to coat. Set aside for later use.

3. In a skillet set over medium to high heat, add in the butter and corn oil. Add in the thinly sliced onions. Cook for 5 minutes or until soft.

4. Add in the chicken mix. Cook for 10 minutes or until the chicken is cooked.

5. Add in half of the coriander and stir well to mix.

6. Add in the heavy whipping cream and stir gently to incorporate. Allow to come to a boil.

7. Remove from heat and garnish with the chopped coriander over the top.

(24) Chicken Karahi

This a modernized version of a popular Pakistani dish I know you will love. Often found being sold from street vendors, this is a dish I know you will want to make as often as possible.

Yield: 6 servings

Cooking Time: 40 minutes

List of Ingredients:

- 3 ounces of butter
- 6 Tablespoons of vegetable oil
- 2 pounds of chicken, cut into small pieces
- 2 teaspoons of garlic, crushed
- 2 teaspoons of ginger, crushed
- 1 pound of tomatoes, chopped
- 1 ½ teaspoons of salt
- 2 teaspoons of powdered coriander
- 2 teaspoons of ground cumin
- Dash of black pepper
- 1 teaspoon of crushed red pepper flakes
- 1 teaspoon of garam masala
- 1 cup of low fat yogurt
- 2 Tablespoons of ground fenugreek
- 3 teaspoons of garlic, thinly sliced
- 6 Tablespoons of green coriander, thinly sliced
- 3 jalapenos, thinly sliced and optional

MMMMMMMMMMMMMMMMMMMMMMMMMMMMMMM

Methods:

1. In a bowl, add in the salt, powdered coriander, ground cumin, dash of black pepper, crushed red pepper flakes and garam masala. Stir well to mix.

2. Rinse the chicken under running water and pat dry with a few paper towels.

3. In a skillet set over medium to high heat, add in the butter and vegetable oil. Add in the chicken pieces. Fry for 8 to 10 minutes or until gold.

4. Add in 1 cup of water and yogurt. Stir well to mix and cook for 3 minutes.

5. Add in the remaining garam masala, ground fenugreek, sliced garlic and sliced green coriander. Stir well to mix. Add in the sliced jalapeno peppers and stir well to incorporate. Cook for 5 minutes.

6. Remove and serve immediately.

(25) Pakistani Samosas

This is a traditional Pakistani snack that you can make whenever you are not in the mood for a full-on meal. Made with a variety of stuffing, you can customize these samosas any way you which.

Yield: 15 to 20 servings

Cooking Time: 55 minutes

Ingredients for the wrapper dough:

- 1 ½ cups of all-purpose flour
- 1 teaspoon of salt
- ¼ cup of shortening
- 6 to 7 Tablespoons of water

Ingredients for the filling:

- ¼ cup of vegetable oil
- ½ cup of onion, minced
- 1 tablespoon of gingerroot, minced
- 1 tablespoon of ground coriander
- 5 russet potatoes, peeled and cooked
- 1 cup of peas
- Dash of salt and black pepper
- Vegetable oil, for frying

MMMMMMMMMMMMMMMMMMMMMMMMMMMMMMMM

Methods:

1. In a bowl, add in the all-purpose flour and dash of salt. Add in the shortening and stir well with your hands until crumbly in consistency.

2. Add in 5 to 6 spoonfuls of cold water and stir well until a pliable dough forms.

3. Set the dough onto a flat surface and knead for 10 minutes or until smooth in consistency. Transfer back into a bowl and cover. Set aside to rest for 30 minutes.

4. In a saucepan set over medium to high heat, add in ¼ cup of vegetable oil. Add in the minced onions, minced gingerroot and ground coriander. Stir well to mix. Cook for 5 minutes or until browned. Remove from heat.

5. In a bowl, add in the cooked potatoes and mash with a potato masher until smooth in consistency with a few chunks in it. Add in the onion mix and peas. Season with a dash of salt and black pepper. Stir well to mix.

6. Place the dough back onto a flat surface and shape into a long rope. Divide the dough into 16 pieces. Roll the pieces out into a 6 inch circle. Slice the circles in half.

7. Fold the cut side together to form a cone shape. Seal the edges with damp fingers.

8. In each cone, add 1 to 2 tablespoons of the filling. Fold the dough over the filling and seal again. Repeat.

9. In a pot set over medium to high heat, fill with 1 to 3 inches of oil. Allow the oil to heat up to 360 degrees. Add in the cones and fry for 5 minutes or until gold.

10. Remove and drain before serving.

About the Author

A native of Indianapolis, Indiana, Valeria Ray found her passion for cooking while she was studying English Literature at Oakland City University. She decided to try a cooking course with her friends and the experience changed her forever. She enrolled at the Art Institute of Indiana which offered extensive courses in the culinary Arts. Once Ray dipped her toe in the cooking world, she never looked back.

When Valeria graduated, she worked in French restaurants in the Indianapolis area until she became the head chef at one of the 5-star establishments in the area. Valeria's attention to taste and visual detail caught the eye of a local business person who expressed an interest in publishing her recipes. Valeria began her secondary career authoring cookbooks and e-books which she tackled with as much talent and gusto as her first career. Her passion for food leaps off the page of her books which have colourful anecdotes and stunning pictures of dishes she has prepared herself.

Valeria Ray lives in Indianapolis with her husband of 15 years, Tom, her daughter, Isobel and their loveable Golden Retriever, Goldy. Valeria enjoys cooking special dishes in her large, comfortable kitchen where the family gets involved in preparing meals. This successful, dynamic chef is an inspiration to culinary students and novice cooks everywhere.

Author's Afterthoughts

Thank you for Purchasing my book and taking the time to read it from front to back. I am always grateful when a reader chooses my work and I hope you enjoyed it!

With the vast selection available online, I am touched that you chose to be purchasing my work and take valuable time out of your life to read it. My hope is that you feel you made the right decision.

I very much would like to know what you thought of the book. Please take the time to write an honest and informative review on Amazon.com. Your experience and opinions will be of great benefit to me and those readers looking to make an informed choice.

With much thanks,

Valeria Ray

Printed in Great Britain
by Amazon